D1131876

Fast Horse Plays
~Round One~

Angeline G. Brom

Executive Series Editor

Fast Horse Drama

Los Angeles, California

Fast Horse Drama is an affiliate of picketfenceforensics.

For more information about purchasing additional copies, please contact
fasthorsedrama@picketfenceforensics.com or refer to www.picketfenceforensics.com

Works in this edition were previously published by picketfencepublications within its
literary magazine:

Mr. Burp, originally published September 2010

Small Mercies, originally published January 2010

Isaac & Rose, originally published January 2011

Keep Them Talking, originally published November 2010

Painting Fires, originally published August 2011

Mortgage and The Inflatable Ship, originally published June 2010

Design and layout by Kevin Davidson

Copyright © 2011 Angeline G. Brom

All rights reserved.

The copyright covers material written expressly for this volume by the author/editor
as well as the works within the compilation itself. Full rights and permissions have
been granted by the authors herein. No part of this book may be reproduced in any
manner whatsoever without the prior written permission of the copyright owner.
Making copies of any part of this book for any purpose other than your own personal
use is a violation of United States copyright laws.

First Edition

ISBN: 0615603688

ISBN-13: 978-0615603681 (Fast Horse Drama)

DEDICATION

With love and affection to Hannah Adams. Although we know you'll never be the next Meryl Streep, we still think you're pretty awesome. You continue to inspire our whole team by reminding us of what hard work and seeking excellence truly mean. Thank you.
And, Y-37, just remember… every round is a final round.

- J, K and A

CONTENTS

ACKNOWLEDGMENTS

Thank you to the playwrights for contributing to this collection and to all of the students who have brought its work to life.

MR. BURP

BY CORA SORENSON

Stella is a verbal and bright nine year old. She often speaks quickly, almost to the point of stumbling over her own words.

STELLA: Gram always said, "He's just as cute as a button," and I always thought that was a really weird thing to say because I've never seen a button that was as cute as he was, but it's just a saying and sometimes sayings don't really make very much sense. Sorry. Sometimes I talk fast when I have a lot to say. Mom says it's because my mind is going fast and my mouth is trying to catch up with it. Which I think is just a nice way of saying I should talk slower. But he was a really neat lizard. His name was George Washington and he was about this big and bright green with little yellow polka-dots. I came home from school one day and he was just lying there and not moving at all. He was dead. I didn't want Mom and Dad to move his cage out of my room, so it just sat there, in the corner for awhile. And I was really sad, but more than anything else, I just wanted to know if GW was going to go to heaven, and I didn't even know if lizards could go to heaven. And then Gram explained to me that when animals...die they go to a place called the Rainbow Bridge and they just play and have fun in this cool place and wait for their people owners to go with them to heaven. It sounded really nice and everything but I wondered if Gram just didn't know and wanted me to feel better. So, I would pray and night and ask God, nicely, if he could just let GW go on to heaven, because I didn't think he should have to wait for me.

And that was about when I started having the Really Bad Dreams. I'm usually pretty okay at explaining things, even if it is in really long sentences, but I don't know how to explain this. I would wake up really late at night and know that I'd just had one of them, but I couldn't remember what it was about. It was like forgetting how to spell a hard word for a test even after you'd written

1

it down a whole bunch of times. I knew that part of my brain knew it, but I couldn't find that part at all. Just things about being cold or a darkness so big that it could swallow you up whole. That doesn't make any sense. It sounds like something a little kid would say, and I'm not a little kid anymore. So in my dream I'd be super scared and I'd be trying to catch my breath and I'd pinch myself and say, "Now you listen, Stella, you wake up right now," and then I would, I'd wake up and I would go and sit in the kitchen with all of the lights on. Until Mom or Dad would come and tell me I should go back to bed.

So, I was having one of these Really Bad Dreams with the big dark and the huge cold and, in my dream, I heard something coming from under my bed. In my dream I'm thinking, "Oh great, this is like one of those monster movies that Gram and I watch, because Mom and Dad won't let me so we have to keep it a secret." But in dreams, you always do the one thing that you should never ever do, so of course I get down on the floor on my hands and knees and I'm looking under the bed and I'm thinking, "This is more scary than any scary movie," and so of course, I'm trying to wake myself up and pinching myself, really, really hard and then I say, "Holy Crud!" because, um, I am awake and this isn't part of the Really Bad Dream anymore, this is a Really Bad Being Awake because my arm hurts cuz I pinched it so hard and under my bed, there's a monster.

And I run as fast as I can downstairs to the kitchen and I turn all of the lights on and Mom finds me there in the morning and she says that maybe my bad dreams are getting worse and I do not say one word about the monster under my bed. I already have a nightmare problem, and I am not going to be the kid with the Overactive Imagination too. Or like Gram says, "Four quarters short of a dollar and headed upstream with no paddles to the booby hatch." Or something like that.

I was so nervous at school the next day that I got two words wrong on my spelling test. I never miss words on my spelling test. I wondered if maybe the monster had escaped from a toxic waste dump, but then I thought about it and there aren't any toxic waste dumps that I know about. Or maybe he was an alien who had come from outer space to test my brain. But I don't really believe in aliens. I decided I was not going to think about him anymore, and anyway, he had probably gone away to hide under some other kid's bed and scare them. Like Janine Martin, because she's mean. That was on a Friday, because we have spelling tests on Fridays, and I had a doctor's appointment.

But he was still there that night and I slept in the kitchen. Mom said I needed to sleep in bed. He was there on Saturday, and I slept in the bathroom. Dad said I needed to sleep in bed. He was there on Sunday night too, and I slept in my closet, where there were no monsters. And I told Mom and Dad about him on Monday, and they told me I had an overactive imagination and that I shouldn't be watching monster movies with Gram. And then Dad looked under the bed with a flashlight, but the monster must not be dumb because he was hiding, and Dad didn't see him. And then Mom sang to me before I went to sleep, which is usually only for little kids, but I made an exception, what with the whole I'm living with a monster under my bed situation. *(She hums a little of Home on the Range.)*

So I thought maybe the monster had gone away to scare Janine until I woke up in the middle of the night and it wasn't because of a Really Bad Dream. It was because, and this is a Very Big "Holy Crud," the monster under my bed was crying. Big, wet, lots of tears and snuffling crying. This was really getting ridiculous. But it's kind of hard to be afraid of a monster who's crying, and when I got down to look under the bed I told him that if he was trying to scare me, he was doing a really bad job. Maybe he was just as scared of me as I was of him. But he looked at me with his big eyes and just kept crying. I was really tired and I had a math test the next day, so I did the one thing a kid should never do with the monster under the bed and that's to tell him he might as well just sleep in bed with me. As long as he stopped crying and didn't snore. Like Gram says, "If you can't beat em, you might as well join em."

And then he was there every night. And he didn't snore at all, but he did burp sometimes. And, um, he was just a really good friend. He was. He didn't make fun of me because I had the special classes at school for the advanced kids, and he wasn't like Mom and Dad who talked about my overactive imagination. He just listened, and I thought I was the luckiest kid ever because the monster under my bed didn't eat me like a chicken mcnugget. He just became my friend. And, um, sometimes kids, even smart kids or strong kids, I think they just need a friend.

I slipped up a couple of times. I did. Talked about Mr. Burp when I was eating my Captain Crunch at breakfast or when my Dad was helping me with my math homework. And they would just smile and laugh, but the thing is, I don't think they understood that I understood. You know? It was like I wanted to explain to them that Mr. Burp wasn't like the Easter Bunny who lays chicken eggs or a fat man who breaks into your house at Christmas. He was just my friend. We talked about how things would be in A Perfect World. Or how a scary monster should come to Janine Martin's house and scare her really bad. Or about my lizard, GW and the Rainbow Bridge. Mom and Dad just didn't really get that, you know? That's okay, though. It really is. I'm not sure if he was something that they could understand.

And so, it wasn't very long ago that I was getting ready for bed- I'd brushed my teeth and everything and I got down to look under my bed and tell Mr. Burp that he could come out for the night and come to bed and um, he wasn't there. And I thought he was just playing hide and seek or something and so I was like, "Okay, Mr. Burp, you can stop hiding now," but then I realized that he wasn't there at all. And I looked all over my room, in my closet, in my dresser, in my cupboards and Mr. Burp wasn't there. And that was when I got really really scared. And I wasn't going to say this, but I started crying because I couldn't find him. And I got panicked. I did. Because Mr. Burp told me that no matter what, he was going to stay with me. And I trusted him. I believed him that no matter how tough things were or how bad I was hurting or how much I just wanted to be a nine year old kid who was happy all the time, he would be there for me. He would be there even though I was sick. I told him that, you know? I told him that and he still didn't go away. So I yelled his name as loud as I could. "Mr. Burp! Mr. Burp! I won't complain anymore. I promise. Please come back, ok? I love you." And I guess I yelled so loud that I woke my Mom and Dad up and they came running out of their room, "I can't find Mr. Burp. I think he went away." And you know what? My Mom started crying, and she held me like I was a little baby. And she just kept saying, "I love you" and I kept saying, "I know, but I need to find Mr. Burp. If he's gone to the Rainbow Bridge already, is he going to wait for me? Am I going to the Rainbow Bridge too?" And you know what? She said he would. He would wait for me if he was there. And she told me that maybe I could make a stop at the Rainbow Bridge on my way to the other place I was going. A place with a lot of light and big pink clouds and...no pain. And I told her I was so scared. Scared for Mr. Burp...and for me. And that I didn't want Mr. Burp to be alone. She told me not to be scared. And she told me that nobody was ever really alone. Ever. I just wish things were different sometimes. *(She hums a bit of Home On the Range.)*

Sorry. I promised Mr. Burp that I wouldn't get weepy. I'm not a little kid anymore. But it's okay, I never really liked my hair anyway. I did like going to school, though. Even if sometimes Janine Martin did make fun of me for going to special classes and reading books that are supposed to be for older kids. Even then. It's hard to go to school when you're just so tired. And when you have to go to so many doctor's appointments that you don't even have time. My doctor is a really nice lady, but I don't think she's used to younger kids asking so many questions or speaking in such long sentences. Like when she delivered the Really Bad News to my parents and not to me. But Mom and Dad told her to just be honest with me, that we would all talk together. I wanted to know what it was called. Acute Lymphoblastic Leukemia. It even sounds scary. That's a name for a really bad monster. Like the kind that probably live in closets. But it's actually the name for a Really Bad Cancer. It's the name for a kind of cancer that kids don't really get better from. I told Mom that I wasn't scared, but I was actually lying a little bit. I feel bad about that because I never ever lie to my Mom, but Mr. Burp told me it was really important for me to be strong for Mom and Dad and Gram. Gram was here yesterday and I told her a secret. I told her that Mr. Burp had come back. That he was here with me and that he just had to go away for a little while to get some things ready. And that he's never going to leave again. And she wasn't surprised at all. I need you to be really quiet, because Mr. Burp is sleeping right now. He told me a secret too. He told me that because he's magic he can go wherever he wants, anytime. Not like people at all. And so he's going to go with me and I don't have to be afraid. I'm not. I did ask God, really nicely, if he could make a little exception and skip that whole Rainbow Bridge part. I'm really looking forward to seeing GW. I just don't want Mom and Dad to be scared. Mom just told me that I'm going to have a

6

little brother. And I told her that I'm going to be watching him from heaven and that I'll be waiting for him to come, when he's like a hundred or something. And Mom said, "I know, sweetheart. I know." I didn't tell Mom, but the cool thing is, Mr. Burp's gonna come and visit him too. I'm just really, really tired. *Home, home on the range. Where the deer and the antelope play.*. I just need to take a little nap. And like Gram always says...

SMALL MERCIES
BY CORA SORENSON

Josephine Smythe, 85, while living in a long term care facility is a sprightly and verbose elderly woman. While her body shows the passage of time, her mind and spirit do not. She is being interviewed about her life by an unseen college student.

I don't know if you'll have quite enough room on that little machine of yours to record all of the stories I could tell you. It's not like I have all that many visitors these days, so I have to take full advantage of the ones that do stop by. Especially when they are as handsome as you are, young man. Now, don't you go blushing on me. My hearing may be failing, but my eyes work just as well as they ever did. Do you have a young lady? I see. You treat her well, young man. You treat her as she deserves to be treated.

My name is Josephine Smythe- you say it "Smith," but you add the "y" and the "e". That's right, it's the British spelling. I was born in 1915 to an American and a Brit in Liverpool. I was one of thousands of war babies, little sail boats headed down a sea of...well, perhaps more like a path, a path of uncertainty. Before I'd finished second grade, my father, the Brit with the very stiff...upper lip, had tired of my very soft mother, the American, and so we were packed up and went to live with my mother's family out in the middle of corn fields on a desert island you may have heard of. Nebraska, they call it. I like to think I kept the best parts of being British- good English and a strong disposition, but also adopted some American sensibilities. You may have noticed my teeth. They're all mine. Never had a filling. Americans know their teeth. They most certainly do. I've gone off and gone on a tangent. Teeth. Ha. You had a question? If I may be so bold, I may need you to speak up, young man.

The secret to happiness? Well, you don't waste any time on pleasantries do you? To whose happiness? Yours? Mine? Now, don't go and start looking all bamboozled again. You look that one up, if you don't know it. I still keep a Webster's next to my bed if you need it. I can't claim to be an expert on anyone else's life but mine. I wouldn't claim it, because I've lived through enough to have a difficult enough time keeping track of my own history. When you've lived to 85, you've earned the right to call it a history, I think. Now, I've gone and gotten myself all tangled up in these grand ideas. It's so nice having a young man to talk to. (beat) No, I assure you. The pleasure is all mine. The secret to happiness is waiting for blue Jell-O. Well, it is. Blue Jell-O is served every Saturday. Not a day before or a day after. And of course, Blue Jell-O is my favorite of all the flavors. I can't for the life of me understand why one would even bother with red or yellow now that they have blue. I enjoy my cup every single Saturday, and then, I begin my wait for the following week. It may sound foolish, but it makes complete sense. It's routine. It's to be expected. And it's a small, but simple pleasure. I do regret that you came today. We don't have any sort of Jell-O on Sunday afternoons because Sunday is pudding day. Why anyone would even consider eating tapioca pudding, I could not tell you.

I fear I may have lost you. I suppose you could say I was speaking in metaphor. My happiness doesn't really hinge on Jell-O, blue or otherwise, dear. Routine. Expecting the expected. There is a comfort in that. Peace, I suppose. I like knowing what to expect. Surprises are...disquieting.

Have you asked her to marry you? (beat.) Your young lady? (beat.) Of course not. You're still in college. It's important to have your ambitions. (beat.) You will always remember your wedding day, but not in the same way that she will, I can guarantee you of that. I was married on May Day, 1935. I had a beautiful white dress and there were so many wonderful flowers. My mother told me that I was the most glorious bride that she had ever seen. And I knew that I was marrying the handsomest man on earth. These film stars that all the young girls go all goofy over these days? Those men couldn't shake a stick compared to my Robert. He held my hand and told me that he would protect me, that he loved me. Oh, and how I loved him. My whole heart was filled up with that love and on that day, I was complete. I was everything I had ever dreamed of being. And he did, he treated me like I was his everything. We lived on the west coast then, and we would go out dancing. We loved jazz music, and he would turn me on the dance floor, and I would close my eyes and let myself fall into him during those minutes. Those trumpets and trombones and clarinets were all playing for me. And he held me, my Robert. It's very difficult to articulate a love quite like that. A love that...

And oh, of course I had my dreams. I thought maybe I could be a nurse or a teacher or even an air hostess, but, you see, I had committed to him, and I agreed to stand behind my word. Because my word was what I had, you see? We wanted, more than anything, to start a family, but it was difficult for me to do so. Oh, can you imagine a woman of my age speaking about this with you? I ask that you don't put that in the interview. Now I've gone and made a bigger issue of it. But we had a little girl, you see. We were blessed with a beautiful baby girl. And my Clara passed two weeks after she was born. Her heart was not fully developed. It was...damaged. She was so precious. Born with a full head of beautiful, thick hair. I had long dark hair when I was younger. And Robert and I would go walking through the gardens in the city, and he knew the scientific names of all of the flowers, and he knew how much I loved the flowers. And we walk through the roses and the gardenias and the rhododendrons and it was like we were dancing again, I could almost hear the piano and the...

I just need a small drink of water. I was injured while carrying Clara. I fell,

13

but. I went...you think this is just the rambling of an old woman four times your age. My mind is as sharp as it ever was, young man. Forgetting would be a small mercy, perhaps. But, then, we are not to forget the things that brought us to our place today, now are we? Any of them? Could you forget the first time you laid your eyes upon..? Did you share her name with me? (beat) Christina. That's a beautiful name. I...how does one speak ill of their one and only? Does that sully the gild of my memory? Once you've gotten me started, I suppose I might simply say it. Let me tell you, I've tried so many times to remember what it was that I had disagreed with Robert about that evening. It was in the summer, and I was several months along with Clara. I don't remember what it was, or I can't, or that part of my brain refuses to. I told him, "No," about something, and he struck me so hard in the stomach that I fell backwards down our staircase.

I do remember the thump-thump-thump of my body as I went down the stairs, like percussion, like this was some sort of dance gone wrong. And I remember, with all that I have to remember with, that it was not so much the physical pain, the pain of my body, that was not what I felt. I felt like the spirit had been struck clean out of me. That was what hurt the most of anything that I could possibly imagine. And so there was a bit of a haze for a few moments there, sort of...sprawled out at the bottom of the stairs, and I went very quickly to a... a very different place altogether, a place where Robert and I were dancing in the middle of a very big garden and he was holding me so close, and I could feel our child inside me, and there was a big band playing and it was like the heavens above us had fulfilled their promise of our happiness, the life I wanted. The life I had expected to have. But I did not get to stay in that place. I looked up and Robert's face was there, above me, but it was not the face I knew. I did not know that he could be that ugly. And I closed my eyes until he made me get up. To see if I was bleeding.

What is the secret to happiness? I could have lost Clara that night, but something much bigger than me made certain that I was able to hold my little girl. That I was able to hold her for 13 days and 7 hours.. Hold her and sing to her, *"Hush little baby, don't you cry..."*
There are small mercies in this life.

How does one continue to love another at their own expense? That would be a question for you, now wouldn't it? I do not know the answer. I know that there were still small moments. Spaces of reprieve, I believe you could call them. Moments in time where I still saw the Robert that I had married, the man I had committed my life to. I did not know how to betray that commitment, and I did not know what had changed in him. It is very important to me that you understand that. And how I needed to believe that it was some failing, some sort of short-coming on my part. I tried to make everything just so. But there is no perfection that is flawless enough to overcome that kind of rage. A wrinkled shirt. A cup of coffee turned cold. A spot on the counter. All insignificant in their own regards and each one enough to inspire vengeance. To bring about the ugliness. His exaggerated consequences for my misdeeds. Broken wrists, arms, toes, ribs. He kicked me until I couldn't breathe. He split my lips so badly I feared that they would never heal. I always went back to the garden, dancing, dancing.. How does a woman forsake her dignity in such a fashion?

I brought two handsome boys into the world. Beautiful, strong, healthy boys. I would like to show you their pictures. And I protected them. It becomes easier to...endure when you have young babies sleeping in the next room over. I would have given everything I had to protect them and keep them safe. It is never enough.

I haven't really left you much room for questions, now have I? (beat.) That's awfully kind of you. Robert left for the war in 1941. I had dreams of leaving with the boys and going somewhere so far away. I thought perhaps I really could become an air hostess and that, somehow I could take the boys with me on the flights, and I would use expensive face powder and lip stain to cover up the bruises, and I would roll the cart down the narrow little aisle and turn to see my boys, strapped into their booster seats, waving at their Mama. Proud of their Mama. Now these really are the rants of an old lady.

Robert wrote me letters while he was away. He was very regular about that. Very routine. And they were wonderful letters.

My Darling Josie,

I would imagine that it's getting to be warm now there. You should take John and Jacob to the gardens and walk with them. We will walk there together, like we used to as soon as I return home. I tell all of the boys that I have the prettiest girl waiting for me back in the plains. I love you, Darling.

Robert.

Dearest Josie,

I do not know that I could live a single day without you. Protect yourself until I can return home.

Robert.

Protect myself? Protect myself? I had to protect myself from you, Robert. I had to believe that I would not be killed at the hand of the man I loved. I had grown terrified you see, of the simplest things, the most everyday, common-place things. Lit cigarettes as instruments of rage. Anything heavy that could be thrown. To bruise. To hurt. To make bleed. The inside of me was bleeding. I loved him so much and yet I felt so useless. So small. The safest I ever was was when you were away. Every night when I went to sleep I dreamt in full color, brighter than any painting. And they were such wonderful dreams, of the life I still believed I could have. I wanted so badly to pretend that he had changed. That he would return home as the man I married. As long as I hold on until next Saturday, they'll be blue Jell-O.

Pardon me? (beat.) Oh. Yes, it was such a cold day for September. It was no Indian summer that year, certainly. The boys were not home from school yet and a man wearing a uniform arrived at our door. *"Ma'am, are you Mrs. Robert Smythe?"*
Why, yes, yes, I'm Josephine Smythe. May I help you?

And I recall that it was so impersonal. So directly to the point, I suppose you could say. *"The United States Army regrets to inform you that your husband, Sergeant Robert P. Smythe lost his life while serving.."*
My husband, but he'll be home soon.. I think you must certainly be mistaken...

I do not precisely know how many emotions can all stand together in a single moment. I do not quite know how I felt just then. I know that I lied down on the floor of our bedroom, and, young man, I wept. I wept for quite a long time. For the years that would not be returned to me. For broken bones and parts of my body that had long since healed and the soul that never would. I wept for Clara and the boys. And most of all I wept because I was happy that my husband would not be coming home. And, because of that, in mind, we could dance forever in the garden, while the band played on and on...

You're a softy aren't you, young man? Christine must quite like that about you. No, I never did. I suspect I felt that it wasn't altogether necessary. I had chosen a man and dedicated my life to him. I didn't feel it was...proper to choose again. I don't mean the world out there, I mean proper for me. And I raised our boys, and time faded most of those memories for them. And I chose dedication through other means. I was a nurse at St. Mary's for 32 years. Always with the babies. I'd liked to think I helped to watch over those littlest of lives. It was very rewarding. I believed very much in the good in this world. There is a lot of good, young man.

You must hold your Christina dear. Treat her like a soft precious metal. And know how strong she is. The secret to happiness is in knowing the small mercies. I don't know how much of this you will choose to share with your father, but I needed to share it with you, my grandson, my Robert. Help an old lady up and let's go take a walk in the garden.

MORTGAGE

A POEM
BY CARL SASOON

idle time does little more than push cracked-up hands
through the hasty wastings of an unused barn door-
i should know, i've been there before,
and before that, it was simply in the past
and there's little to no need for me to bore you
with crucial details, but, if you'll bear with me,
you'll come to understand how i can't heal you.
how many hours i'll find myself trying, though.
unavoidable instruction, much like cold bruises
or broken tractors or the factoring in that i found
myself doing when i started in with the ugly business
of losing you.

i suppose i should drive on into town and see about
having a cast put on it.

what exactly do they in this sort of circumstance?
slide you open, reach wide inside and replace what's
rotten with something somebody else should've forgotten.
i need a broken heart like the crops need rain
and this is the same thing that happened when we fogged
the fields. take away the life but keep on with the living.
i warned you,
i could stretch the clichés so thin i could dress myself in them.
if i had the energy, the believing in something big,
the good excuse for letting go.

slow, slow. easy does it, for fear this old ticker
will get all wild and insist on doing that
awful blistering thing again.
no, there's not a Goddamn thing Dr. Johnson
can do about this terrible business.

i suppose i should walk on into town and see about
having it taken out.

you get some very nice sympathy gifts
if you're brave enough to tell folks that it just went missing.

with your help,
i'll pull the columns together, add the numbers up right and
gee golly gosh darn
i'll be able to go ahead and make this month's payment.
brown crops yield no good fruit
and things got awfully crazy when we had to start
in with shooting all of the cattle.
and they were right on the money with what they
said about going into the slaughterhouse business.
they look at you like they know you and you
smile hard and then you blow them away.
eyes like vacant memories, flying saucers,
an unauthorized abduction.
soft meat yields hard cash,
but only an uncivilized person eats someone
when he's still alive, still warm, or still breathing.

i could keep doing this, you know.
i could survive the executions,
just the same as i surmised your
hold-me-up games with the farm boys,
the fucking around with the barley,
that nice time you insisted i dance with the shovel.
rubble left,
things have gone missing-
but i'm really just so thrilled with how much weight i've lost.

i suppose i should crawl on into town and see about
someone putting me out of my mercy.

someday very soon, a man dressed all in black
really will roll up here and he will say

i have to do a short salute. i have to give my farm back.
you will be a good audience. you will boo and hiss
but i mustn't miss what i will commit to not remembering.
i will wear a bandana to cover up the blood.
i will do you no favors, i will singlehandedly
recalculate our heavy, ice cold mortgage.
i will praise the chasteness of corn fields
because sheep say cluck-cluck,
and pigs say moo-moo,
and while holding my hands out to show that they are empty,
i say,
i only did what i had to do.

ISAAC & ROSE
BY JARED BOTICELLI

ISAAC appears before the audience, smiles and mouths, silently, "I love you, forever." and then transitions to

ROSE who adjusts the microphone stand in front of her, adjusting it's height, before tapping the microphone and saying

Is this thing on? *(beat)* That was a joke. Funny, huh? Ok, well, maybe not. I thought it was. You know, make some jokes, warm my audience up a little bit. Maybe I could be like a stand-up Helen Keller. Well, I can talk though. Sort of. *(speaks very slowly and with much exaggeration)* Can you understand me? You're nodding, so I guess that's a yes. Let me tell you the biggest joke, though. The fact that I'm the one up here talking about him. I mean, how long's it been? Well, I could tell you to the day. 407 days since. All of them long. Every one. But they asked that I come and talk about him and I... I don't do very well with excuses. I just tell it like it is. I'm deaf, but I'm not stupid. *(beat)* That was another joke. Ha. ha. ha. The deaf older sister pays tribute to her genius little brother. They would call that poetic irony, right? Something like that. *(She stares out into the audience again, fiddles a little with her mic.)*

They asked me to talk about him. To tell you about him, so that's what I'm going to do. He started playing when he was three. Really. Would climb right up onto the stool and he would stare at the keys like he was studying them or something, and he would make up little songs. I was eight, almost nine then, and these things *(she motions to her ears, indicating her hearing aids)* still worked a little. I could make out some of it. The songs. The things he was able to do with the piano by the time he was five, six, seven. Our parents both played, not like that, but they played and by then they were letting him listen to Wagner, Tchaikovsky, Bartok. By this time, I heard less and watched more. How about a nine year old how can play Rachmaninoff's 3rd Concerto? Ha.

His hands were too small to play those big octaves, so he would... *(she motions crossing her hands over each other, as if playing.. she closes her eyes..)* Isaac.. that was the last piece I can remember being able to hear him play.

Jokes. Yes, we, well, I, I was talking about jokes. Maybe God likes to do experiments sometimes and see how good he can make someone. How right. How correct. I'm supposed to be talking about Isaac and I am. I am. Like this perfect little person. Sitting at that big black piano, he looked like a little doll sometimes, like that big piano could just swallow him up whole. Fold up on him or something. Or the math he did in his head. Foreign languages. And he sang and they tested him when he was, I don't know, seven or so, his IQ... *(her voice sort of fades off and she gazes out into the audience, perhaps as if she sees him.)* Well, I'm deaf, but I'm not dumb. But how do you compete with that, right? So to be all of that, to have that kind of talent and then to be that.. that... good. A good person. Humble. Kind. Let's say something about my personality. Bitter. Angry. Impatient. Then think of the opposite and that's Isaac. It is. As if the weight of his gifts was only bearable through humility. I think I was in fifth grade when my teacher told me, "You are so smart, Rose. So smart. But you are so angry." Yeah, and you can fuckin' hear, lady. Get off it. Try to help the little deaf, antisocial girl. They are not going to make a movie about you. Ha. That was a joke.

(She clears her throat. Appears to recompose herself.) Jealousy is a bitter, toxic disease. A poisonous weed that grows without end. I am it's victim. Powerless to it. A disease worse than the fever that screwed up ears when I was a baby or that shut down my.. *(she gestures at her torso, towards her right kidney)* well, we will get to that. To really talk about Isaac I think I have to talk about me. At least I live up to the hype. *(A small, mirthless laugh and then she speaks quickly, almost garbling her words)* Self-consumed. Self-involved. Self-centered. Self. Self. Self.

Self. Do we see a pattern here? At least I could read early, and I could read all the crap that they wrote about me. Or maybe just jealous. We were fighting well, not fighting, because he didn't do that. I was being a horrible fifteen year old, throwing a fit.. he was ten, I'd had some crap happen at school and I was angry, like always and he told me *(ROSE transitions to ISAAC and mouths, "I understand you."* then, a beat..) I understand you. And I told him. I told him you don't. I...God, I pushed him into the pool. *(She gestures as if holding ISAAC under the water)* I did. I pushed him under the water. He was so small. And I, I held him there. I didn't let him up. I yelled at him while I held him under there. I yelled, "Do you, Isaac? Do you "understand" me? This is how it is. Can you hear me? You little punk." *(she gestures releasing him. She lets out a long, slow breath.)*

And I let him up. He was okay. Shaken up. But he was okay. My parents, always the loving, supportive mother and father, comforting us both. And he said, "I love you, Rose. I love you, big sister." No. You don't. You shouldn't. Maybe if I'd had the guts to...

He drew a picture of us. We're sitting on a piano bench on the beach, and you can see the ocean in the background. He's playing and I'm looking out towards the waves. White and powerful. We look happy. People are rarely happy. Maybe God makes more mistakes than we want to admit. *(Another steady, long breath before she refocuses on the audience.)*

High fevers. Crap ears. Inside parts that don't work very well. My parents should have asked for a refund. Or at least an upgrade. I guess that's why they got Isaac. Good for them. They deserved him. I mean that. For every award that Isaac won, I had a new doctor or a new issue that needed attention. And, well, then the big one hit. The one that couldn't just be fixed by a doctor. The kidneys main job is to remove the waste- the toxins- out of the blood and mine were just really tired of doing that. First they went on strike and then they quit with very little notice, only to come back part time, sort of. Unreliable. *(She gestures towards her left kidney, touching her torso.)* And then the left one gave up altogether. The right one wasn't far behind. *(She holds her side and pauses)* They put you on a list. And they tell you to stay strong and be patient. Which is great advice while your internal organs betray you and your body rots. And you spend a lot of time feeling sorry for yourself, and most of the time you're angry and sick, and sometimes you yell at your little brother when he lies down next to you, and you drum your fists over his back like a crazy ass, and then sometimes you let him curl up next to you and feel his heartbeat. *(She gasps, suddenly and unexpectedly.)* And you pray to God to be forgiven and to be changed into a better person, and if he can't do that then maybe he should consider ending your miserable existence. And you watch your little brother play the piano and you wish, you wish that you could hear him. And your number never comes up. It never does. Crappy body. Rarest blood type. Poetic irony.

A call comes at 2 am one night. I'm rushed to the hospital. Gotten ready for surgery. The kidney isn't *(she pronounces it slowly, carefully, deliberately)* viable. That's a shock. Neither is my life. Our parents take us to the beach. I try to be decent, I do. I do. But I just keep thinking that it's like a Lifetime movie about the angry, dying deaf girl who gets taken to the seaside by her loving parents and genius little brother and they all bond and she becomes Pollyanna and... I'm no Pollyanna. And that's all a big bunch of bull crap. Isaac and I were both silent and we were walking along the beach and he told me *(she silently mouths, You're my hero. You are.)* And I told him *(she speaks with anguish, as if she can barely get the words out)*, "No, Isaac. I'm not. I'm not anybody's hero. I am so angry. You have everything. Everything." And I ran as fast as a sick girl can over the beach, leaving him standing there, a teenager now, but small, like he could still be ten or something. He didn't run after me. No. He just stood there, looking out over the sand towards the water. But he didn't have any piano like that picture he drew. And neither of us were smiling. Life sucks compared to the movies. People are rarely truly happy. *(She pauses and then smiles, almost garishly)* Two gnomes walk into a bar. This isn't really a time for jokes.

And then, suddenly, soon after the time at the beach, my number did come up again. Ding ding ding. That's how it sounds, right? And it's early morning, the sun is coming up and it's just my Dad and I driving to the hospital. And he says some things on the way but he's talking ahead, he's driving, so I can't see his lips, but his eyes water and he looks older than before. And I think, all of this because of me. Every bit of it. And it seems so unfair. It does. And they suit me up and I go in and, after a while, I'm floating into a place with dark, black pools of liquid and I'm dreaming that my ears are perfect again and I'm listening to Isaac play- the third Rach, of course- and I'm floating or flying or something and then my body goes heavy and I give way to the darkest sleep. *(She pauses and closes her eyes, placing her hands at her side, near her kidney. Her eyes open.)*

You awake through a dark fog of red and black, you go back to the sleeping place a few times. A nurse is trying to sign at me *(she signs a bit with her hands)* through the fog ,and her hands are weak. My parents are there, in chairs in the corner. *(She speaks quickly again, almost as though she is reliving the recovery from surgery, words are a mish mash..)* Both are crying. And it's the loudest sobbing, although I can her nothing but the huge silence. My mouth is filled with stones. My side aches. My body is invaded. I will sleep for years. I will awaken as heavy as the deaf gargoyle. I go, wake and sleep, sleep and wake, through sunset, night, sunrise. My mouth is dry as sand, but I can barely drink. I choke. I awaken, head better but still hurting. Mom and Dad are at my bedside. Their faces are broken puzzles. I ask for Isaac.

Even though I do not understand, I know. I can not hear, but I can feel. I am shaking my head like a fish removed from water. I ask for Isaac. My brother. My Isaac. They are both crying now, and it's like a boiling river inside of me, because I feel him there and I can not survive this. I will die right here. Now. I thrash so hard that the IV rips from arm, and I'm on the floor and it's the three of us there and they are holding me, and I'm three again with a fever so high that I'm burning up, a field of fire, a desert of flames, and we're on the floor, and I wonder if a river of tears could carry us away, out to the ocean and will we find Isaac there, whole, unharmed. He is smiling. I sleep. I hope to not awaken. *(She pauses again. Recovers from her tears. Prepares to speak again.)*

Isaac knew that I would have said no, would have fought it physically if I'd known. He was right. God has a strange sense of humor sometimes. My parents didn't even try to talk him out of it. They respected him and they never blamed me. I don't really know how that's even possible. He had a reaction to the anesthesia and he..um, he went to sleep. He was fifteen years old. And this is what's left *(she gestures down, at her side.)* This is the part of him that he gave so that I could stay alive. I did nothing to deserve this. How did his heart hold all of that love? Does this *(gestures again)* give me just a little of that? What do I do with it? Where do you go from here? *(beat)* A great movie of the week. *(beat)* Is this thing on? *(a short, mirthless laugh.)*

I wonder sometimes about how it feels about being inside of here. Does it long for its original owner? Does it feel as angry as I do sometimes? Will I awaken some cold night to the bursting of my skin, the leaping free, the escape from misery. I want to do right by him. I fear that I cannot be forgiven. What was Isaac's last thought as he slipped into that sleep? Fear? Anger? Regret? Maybe I cannot understand that generosity of spirit. Maybe I am incapable of it. Isaac gave me his kidney, but he kept his heart. Unmatched. Oh God... *(She has to pause and look out over her audience again.)*

So thank you all for coming here today, for him. But he wasn't much for taking credit. He got nervous before he performed. He was shy. He was very humble. He didn't show anyone his art. I have a few of the drawings. He was kind. He was the strongest and most beautiful person I have ever known and I am trying to be a better person, a good person, to.. *(pause)* honor him. If I hadn't been so angry, so unwilling to be happy, maybe I would have had time to explain to him how much I loved him. Thank you, Isaac.   I love you, brother. I love you forever and ever and ever. And I'm sorry. Remember how we took some lessons together and then I just quit like I did with everything. At least I had the excuse of being almost deaf. I'm trying again. And I'm remembering what you told me. You knew so much for a little kid. You told me, even though something is tough, it doesn't mean it's impossible. Anything is possible. Yeah. I guess so. So, anyway, I'm trying. It's hard but I'm trying. Even if I can play just a few things. *(Suddenly she's embarrassed. She stops.)* So, thank you all for coming today, we have a video of Isaac playing and several of his drawings and paintings are.. *(Her voice fades...)*

ISAAC appears and mouths quietly, "I love you, forever."

ROSE: I love you forever too, little brother.

31

KEEP THEM TALKING
BY CRAIG SHAFER

Rocky and Kip work the paramedic graveyard shift. In their mid 20's, they've known each other for years and are close friends.

KIP: Dude, you're sleeping.

ROCKY: *(awakening from half sleep)* No, not sleeping. Just resting my eyes.

KIP: While snoring?

ROCKY: I don't snore.

KIP: You do snore and you were sleeping. You promised you wouldn't sleep.

ROCKY: It just seems like wasted energy. There's two of us here. That means one of us, namely, you, can busy yourself while waiting in a heightened state of alertness for our next call to heroics and I can busily.. study the backs of my eyelids.

KIP: We'll drive over to 7-11 and you can busy yourself with a Mountain Dew.

ROCKY: *(drowsy again)* No more Mountain Dew. Kills the soldiers. Maybe a Red Bull.

KIP: I don't want to think about your soldiers, dude. Besides, it's not like they have any battle prospects on the horizon.

ROCKY: I dunno, I-

KIP: Mountain Dew got you through your boards. Red Bull tastes like Baby Aspirin. It's disgusting.

ROCKY: *(out of nowhere, he suddenly sings..)* "I did the Dew and Kip was busy staring at my shoe, who knew"

KIP: Okay, freak-a-zoid, if you ever want to give up saving people's lives, I'm sure you have a promising future in show tunes. If you're gonna do that, maybe you should go back to sleep.

ROCKY: I wasn't

KIP: You were.

ROCKY: Ok, then, say it

KIP: Rocky

ROCKY: Say it, just say it

KIP: Fine, whatever. We taped the codes to the bottom of your converse so I could read them while we were taking the boards. Do you want me to get out and announce it over a megaphone on Broadway. *(He acts this out, with exaggeration)* Attention, world, I was too distracted to study for the paramedic boards, so my best friend Rocky helped me cheat. Thank you, world, that is all. Happy?

ROCKY: Perhaps I could choreograph a little dance routine, write a song, *(singing, with the same tune as before)* "Hello world..

KIP: Has it ever occurred to you that all of your songs have the exact same melody?

ROCKY: *(again, with the same tune, but maybe a slight variation)* This is a little song about my best friend Kip

KIP: Enough, dude. I get it.

ROCKY: You don't need to be salty about it.

KIP: I'm not being salty. I just don't need to be reminded about it on a weekly basis.

ROCKY: I didn't mean it like that. I'm sorry. I'm on edge tonight. You're a great medic. You know that. And you were distracted. I mean,

RADIO: *(the dispatcher interrupts)* Unit 76, we have a code 24 on the 1600 block of Hamilton. Caucasian female, 30's, in traffic, distressed and agitated, respond 12

KIP: Why do slow nights always mean a Psych call? Either there's a whole lot of crazy in this town or the universe is torturing us. I'd rather be water boarded.

ROCKY: You're a great medic, dude. I mean it.

KIP: Thanks for the encouragement, skipper. At least you're not sleeping

ROCKY: I wasn't sleeping. I was resting- *(he sees a woman in traffic and motions)* she's over there. Bright mumu at eleven o'clock.

KIP: Well, Aloha. Here, jump out.

ROCKY: *(getting out of the truck and approaching the woman)* Ma'am, come over here with me, please, out of the way of traffic. My name is Rocky, what's your name, Ma'am?

BURGER QUEEN: I am the Burger Queen and you are my son, the beautiful Prince of all Burgers.

ROCKY: Actually, no, Ma'am, I'm a paramedic, but, really, I'm flattered. Can you sit down with me here? *(He sits with the Burger Queen and, to Kip)* Kip, can you call in a 1705?

BURGER QUEEN: Have you ever been to Madagascar? My husband, the Burger King is being held there as a political prisoner. In his absence, I rule these lands.

ROCKY: Right, and my Godfather just happens to be the Easter Bunny. Where do you live, ma'am?

BURGER QUEEN: In a far away castle built of beautiful, glistening, golden french fries.

ROCKY: Residence unknown. Alright, ma'am,

KIP: I've actually been more of a whopper guy myself

BURGER QUEEN: *(exclaiming)* Heathen. Dirty, filthy heathen. Ronald is a pervert!

ROCKY: Now, that's a little harsh, don't you think?

KIP: Ma'am, if you could just get in the car with this nice lady, she's a policewoman and she's going to take you over to All Saints. *(they help the Burger Queen to the police car)*

BURGER QUEEN: You are my Prince. I will call you Whopper Junior!

ROCKY: And I'll be grateful that the cops in this town get the privilege of taking in the crazies. Why can't they just respond to the calls too?

KIP: The world just doesn't make much sense, Rock.

ROCKY: Point for the Kipster. Hey, you know, I wanted to show you something. I've had it for a couple of days, and well, I figured I would tell you first. Brothers from another mother and all that. *(he reaches into his pocket)*

KIP: This sounds big. Please tell me it's not a terminal cancer diagnosis. I can't do Lifetime movie tonight.

ROCKY: Can it. No, this is actually good. This is me actually taking a stand for once.

KIP: I'm filled with heated anticipation.

ROCKY: Apparently. *(taking out a small box, he shows it to Kip)* Look. *(he opens the box and removes a ring)*

KIP: What the hell is that?

ROCKY: Well, Kip, the small velvet box may have been your first clue. Now, if you'll look at this shiny band. In our culture, when a guy is preparing to confess his undying-

KIP: -Dude, I'm just not that into you

ROCKY: Hysterical. Kip, this is it. Big time. Serious. I'm really doing it. I'm going to propose to Julia.

KIP: You're going to what?

ROCKY: I'm going to ask Julia to marry me, man.

KIP: Are you kidding me?

ROCKY: Nope. Serious as a Code 6 Cardiac Arrest. I've waited long enough. I'm ready. She's ready. We're all ready. I should write a song about this, *(singing, big, show tune style, but as always, with the same tune)* "I'm ready, She's ready, we're..

KIP: Same tune, dude. I am so completely lost. I thought you guys were taking a break, waiting to see how things worked out. Spreading your wings.

ROCKY: My wings are done spreading. I want to settle down. It's time, Kip. I've always known she was the one. I just needed to get up the guts to tell her. Well, I mean, I've always known since I met her when she was dating you and you dumped her after a month.

KIP: *(flatly, and with a small sadness)* I didn't dump her.

ROCKY: Well, whatever, went your separate ways, but, anyway, that's ancient history, it's done, forgotten. I'm ready to ask her to be my wife. I want you to be my best man. Maybe we'll have a dance routine. So, what do you say?

KIP: Um, congratulations. When are

RADIO: *(the dispatcher interrupts them)* Code 2 at 829 Cannon Avenue. Male, 42, Unit 76, location?

ROCKY: 4 minutes, tops. Dude, you are going to look sweet in a tux! Maybe Jules'll invite that one girl you kind of liked. Mariel? Do guys get a chance to catch the bouquet? How does that work?

KIP: I'm not sure, Rocky.

ROCKY: *(singing again)* "Whose wedding day is it? It's my wedding day!" *(looking for the house number)* Which one is 829?

KIP: *(Kip sees an injured man in his driveway)* I dunno, maybe this one, with the dude standing in the garage holding a blood soaked towel to his hand. Just a wild guess. I'm parking in the driveway. He doesn't look terminal.

ROCKY: *(getting out, and approaching the man)* Evening, sir. I'm Rocky

CABINET MAN: And that's Bullwinkle? Sorry. Bad time. Bad Joke.

KIP: Kip. What happened, Sir?

CABINET MAN: I've been using this band saw, working on new kitchen cabinets for my wife. She's a little demanding, boys. And I'm not the best with power tools. And well, before I knew it, I'd taken a finger off.

CABINET MAN'S WIFE: *(from off stage, we can not see her. Voiced by Kip.)*

Chuck? Ch-ch-chuck? Are my cabinets done? Who are you talking to out there? I don't think you should be talking to anyone if my cabinets aren't done!

CABINET MAN: Sorry, honey. Still working on them!

ROCKY: Wow. Bummer. Glad you called 911 immediately, sir. Come on..

CABINET MAN: I didn't.

KIP: You didn't?

CABINET MAN: Oh no, that was three or four hours ago. I think. I'm sorry, I'm feeling a little woozy.

ROCKY: You cut off your finger and you didn't go to the emergency room?

CABINET MAN'S WIFE: Chuck? Ch-ch-chuck? Where in the hell are my cabinets? Where do you think you're going exactly?

CABINET MAN: I'm sorry, honey. I'm bleeding pretty badly.

ROCKY: Sir?

CABINET MAN: Sorry. Yes. I cut the first finger off and then, well, two more, I think. Or maybe it's three. *(he begins to unwrap the bandage)*

KIP: No need to check, Chuck.

ROCKY: *(he notices Cabinet Man's foot, also bleeding and bandaged)* Your foot, sir?

CABINET MAN: After all the ruckus with my hands, I was using my foot to steady the board and well, a couple of toes..

CABINET MAN'S WIFE: Ch-ch-chuck!

KIP: Let's go, Chuck. *(they load him into the ambulance)*

ROCKY: *(to the dispatcher)* Unit 74, coming in with the code 2. Um, multiple..digits..stable. Arrival in 5 to 7. Chuck, I was just telling Kip that I'm getting ready to propose to my girl.

CABINET MAN: Best decision you'll ever make.

KIP: No doubt.

ROCKY: *(looking around)* Where's your bag, Kip? I need more compresses.

KIP: Sorry, dude. I completely forget it when I left tonight. We can pick up an extra at Saints.

ROCKY: Steady breaths, Chuck. You're gettin' a little shocky on me.

CABINET MAN: I just wish I could have finished the cabinets.

KIP: It's one of those comes in threes nights. I can feel it.

ROCKY: We don't really save people's lives.

KIP: Say what? Are you about to get all philosophical on me?

ROCKY: Well, we don't. We drive around in a flashing, beeping short-bus mostly responding to cuckoos who don't have the where-with-all to go to the hospital. Smart people take themselves to the hospital.

KIP: You're a smart guy, Rocky.

ROCKY: Huh? Well, I'd take myself to the ER, that's for sure. I mean, sometimes we get somebody who actually is hurt or whatever, but really, the most we do is just keep them talking. Keep them company while we drive like we have since we were 16.

KIP: I was actually 15 when I got my license. As you remember.

ROCKY: Jack ass.

KIP: The truth hurts.

ROCKY: You're a dork, but you're my best friend. I mean, I'm kind of a dork.

KIP: Rocky, I...

RADIO: *(the dispatcher interrupts them)* Code 24 on Old Brewster Rd, mile stop 4. Unit 76, location?

KIP: I'd like to say three hours, but that would be a lie.

ROCKY: 10 minutes, tops.

RADIO: Disoriented elderly female, 70's to 80's. Motorist with her, but she's refusing to go.

KIP: We're on our way. There she is. I'm going to try to figure out where we're taking her back to, if you want to calm her down and get her into the.. short bus.

ROCKY: *(he approaches the woman)* Beautiful evening, isn't it, ma'am? Must be a little chilly without your coat.

STAR LADY: No, it's lovely. I just went for a walk to look up at the stars. And then this man came along and tried to either rape or kidnap me! Or both. I think he's probably an alien.

ROCKY: I think he was just concerned about you, ma'am, but I suppose you can never be too cautious. *(to the unseen man)* Thank you, sir. We've got her.

STAR LADY: So many stars. So many aliens up there.

ROCKY: Why don't you come with me over to the ambulance. Do you see a lot of aliens, ma'am?

STAR LADY: Don't be daft, young man, I don't see them. I'm not a loon. I just know they're up there. *(Rocky is helping Star Lady into the ambulance)*

ROCKY: Makes sense.

STAR LADY: I love you too, William.

ROCKY: Excuse me?

STAR LADY: I'm sorry, I was talking to William.

ROCKY: Are you hearing voices, ma'am?

STAR LADY: Of course I am. Doesn't everyone?

ROCKY: Well, what are the voices saying now?

STAR LADY: They are saying.. let's see.. "Well, what are the voices saying now?"

ROCKY: Okay, you got me. I'm sorry.

STAR LADY: I'm a dotty old lady who misses her husband, young man, but I'm not a coconut ball.

ROCKY: A coconut ball?

STAR LADY: I'm allergic to nuts. Don't care much for the phrase. I miss him the most at night. After fifty-four years of marriage, I don't think the heart ever recovers quite right. It's just broken.

ROCKY: We're going to take you home ma'am.

STAR LADY: Thank you. I did walk quite a ways tonight.

KIP: *(to the dispatcher)* Unit 76, we're heading over to White Street, call on the 24, all clear. No injuries.

ROCKY: Just rest tight, ma'am.

KIP: Rocky, I wanted to tell you that

ROCKY: *(interrupting)* Do you think I'll be married for 54 years? I can't even imagine 54 years, seriously. *(a particularly soulful little ditty)* "Oh, If I was 83, I'd always have to pee and I'd be withered like a tree.."

KIP: Lame. Worse rhymes than usual. And same tune.

ROCKY: I know.

KIP: Maybe we're done for tonight. We can hope.

ROCKY: There's always hope.

KIP: Usually.

ROCKY: No, always I think.

KIP: Have you thought about going back to school? Med school, I mean. Actually saving people? You could do it, you know. Even with the singing.

ROCKY: I think that ship has sailed, my man. I don't want all that. I don't want to be good at that. I want to be good at having a family. Good at being with Julia. Good at just being me.

KIP: I think you'd be a good doctor, Rock.

ROCKY: And I think you're a great medic. We've been through this.

RADIO: *(the dispatcher interrupts them)* Code 20 on Chandler Avenue. Address and apartment number are incoming.

KIP: 76 is headed over.

ROCKY: Wow. An overdose. Goth kid drank some drano? Bored housewife took one too many Percocet? I'm not sure if tonight can get any better. What time is it?

KIP: 4:15.

ROCKY: Julia and I are having dinner tonight.

KIP: I k- *(Rocky interrupts him from saying, I know)*

ROCKY: I'm gonna do it tonight. The ring. The proposal, I mean.

KIP: Rocky, I

RADIO: Building at 1620 Chandler, apartment number forthcoming.

ROCKY: Holy crap, it's Jules' building. I mean, it's a huge building, but what are the chances? Maybe I'll just end my shift after this one, if you'd be okay with doing the drive.

KIP: Well, yeah, I mean, of course.

ROCKY: Maybe I'll just do it over breakfast or something.

RADIO: Code 20 is at 1479.

ROCKY: What?

RADIO: Repeating, Code 20 at unit 1479.

ROCKY: *(frantic)* WHAT? No, that's wrong. Confirm. NOW. Confirm.

RADIO: The code 20 is at unit 1479.

KIP: We have it. We'll be there in two.

ROCKY: No. no. no. no. It's wrong. They're wrong. It's a mistake. It's just a silly mistake. That's Julia's building, I

KIP: I kn-

ROCKY: Will you hurry the hell up? What the hell is wrong with you, Kip? Park there. Just park there.

KIP: *(they are unloading and heading up)* Listen to me. Just calm down, okay? You won't be able to help like this.

ROCKY: Calm down? You want me to calm down? Is that a joke? Come on. Now.

KIP: *(Kip arrives first and finds Julia)* The door's open. It's her, Rocky. It's her. I need you to start breathing and calm down.

ROCKY: *(Rocky gets down and begins taking vitals while talking to Julia)* Baby. Baby. Baby. Jules. Julia. Honey, honey, can you hear me? Okay, she's breathing. Shallow, but she's breathing. Pulse, take the pulse. Honey, what did you do. What did you do? You're gonna be fine, you're gonna be just fine.

KIP: *(Kip is looking at a pill bottle)* Rocky, I..okay, *(together, they are lifting Julia onto the stretcher)* let's get her up, we'll have her there within 10 minutes, she's gonna be fine.

ROCKY: Kip. *(He picks something up. A bag. He shows it to Kip)* What's that?

KIP: What are you talking about? We don't have time for this. Let's go.

ROCKY: What the fuck is that, Kip? Why is your medic bag on Julia's living room floor? Kip? No, this is a bad dream. This is a very bad dream. A very, very bad dream. And I'm going to wake up and just start singing and everything will just be fine. Let's go.

KIP: *(They are loading Julia into the ambulance)* I'm with you. I got her. We'll be back to the truck in two. She's been struggling. She's been..we've been..

ROCKY: Why is your goddamn bag in Julia's apartment, Kip? Tell me, Kip. Please tell me..

KIP: I am so sorry, Rocky. I tried to

ROCKY: You are sorry. You are nothing to me. How long, Kip? How long.

KIP: I asked her to marry me.

ROCKY: Just stay with me, baby. This is all some big mistake. Yeah, I hear you, honey, just stay with me.

KIP: I wanted to tell you.

ROCKY: I don't hear you. Stay with me, baby.

KIP: It's been over for her for awhile. She wanted to tell you. We wanted to tell you. So it wouldn't come to this.

ROCKY: There is no we, Kip. Baby, just stay with me.

KIP: I didn't mean for you to find out like this.

ROCKY: There is nothing to find out. Julia is going to be my wife and you are nothing. You are nothing. Nothing. Nothing. Nothing.

KIP: She doesn't love you anymore, Rocky.

ROCKY: Just keep talking, baby. Just stay with me.

KIP: *(to dispatcher)* Unit 74, incoming with the code 20. Stable. Vital signs are fair.

PAINTING FIRES
BY COLE SUTTERLAND

PAINTER: That is so nice of you. I get a little funny about my work, I guess, and, I don't know, flustered or something. Have you been a couple of blocks down the sidewalk? There's some amazing, really amazing painters here. No, I, mean. That's very sweet of you, but these are just pictures of my life. If I haven't seen it, I can't paint it. I remember hearing that old saying about "write what you know," and I'm a terrible writer, so I guess I just "paint what I know." There isn't anything very special about it.

This is, um, where my son and I go to find our Christmas tree every year. Sort of single mom, have to know how to use a saw. I never did a very good job, and I would always tell my son, "I guess that's what dads are for," and he would laugh. He always names the trees and them and holds a little service to honor their passing when New Year's comes. I can't remember the tree's name that year. Or what my son got me...he always asks for the funniest things, though. Kids, you know. A book of maps. A new collar for his puppy. A tape recorder. What kid asks for a tape recorder for Christmas? We don't have much, so.. No, no, it's not sunset, there's just a bit of smoke or something on the horizon. Fire season. Oh, thank you so much. It's just a painting of our house. Blue and white. Small. Simple. But very happy. Like our lives, I guess you would say.

I'm so sorry. It's not for sale. No, I, I just can't. That's very generous of you, but it isn't finished yet. I'm sorry. That's of my son and his dog, Buddy. Big mutt. My son was walking home from school one day and just like in the movies, Buddy followed him home. And he stayed. Right by Buddy's side. He does look sad there, I guess. He should be happy, warm by the fireplace, with his master. I guess, well, you see, we had been living with someone, we aren't, now, but we were then, and he didn't like Buddy barking. It annoyed him, he said. I stood my ground, though. And Buddy stayed. He stayed...forever. My son's father died when he was a baby and it was just the two of us for years. And we were very happy. I sang to my son every night before he went to sleep. His favorite was the one about the..the...picnic..do you know that one? But then, when I met John, I thought that...I'm sorry, I'm rambling, I know, I just, I'm trying to explain about the painting of the house.

I met John and, at first, he did all of the right things. Flowers for me. Little league games with my son. And then, well, I guess sometimes things change so slowly that you don't even realize it until it's too late. And then you get stuck, I guess. Yeah, it's a forest fire. Nature's version of a do-over. The fire splits open the cones and they say that the trees grow back stronger and taller. But it takes a long time. So, I got stuck. John would come home from work and his nights were spent in front of the TV. He brought a permanent winter with him and we didn't really speak much anymore. It was like my son became an imposition, like a gnat that one might bat away out of annoyance. Angry words. Cold stares. I love my son very much. We didn't spend much time at home anymore. I brought that winter into our home and I let him stay. I'm sorry, I'm boring you, babbling on like this.

I love that one too. Yeah, it's my son after the spelling bee. We spent hours in the evenings, just the two of us, on long drives practicing for it. I've never seen a ten year old so dedicated to something. I couldn't believe it. Words that felt like they were thirty letters long and he would just go over and over them. He only missed one word, right at the end. I was so excited. I was holding my breath. I was just so proud of him though. I..I'm sorry, I don't remember the word exactly. It was...I don't even really remember what it meant, that word.

Oh, I would love for you to meet him too. That would be wonderful. No, I don't think he'll be able to come down tonight. I've been waiting, but... He's with Buddy, somewhere. No, no. I don't think I'm a very good mother at all. Oh. I don't know if I can finish the picture of the house tonight. I'm so sorry. I...well. I can't finish it because I still don't know how that story ends.

I guess, I didn't want us to be stuck anymore, you see. I was only going to be gone for just a little while. Just a bit. And, I.. left my son and Buddy, they were watching TV in the living room and John, he was asleep on the couch, just like he always was. And I kissed my son on the top of his head and told him I'd be right back. Just right back. So, a little while later, my son, he calls me and he tells me that Buddy had started barking at John and well, John had told my son to "go upstairs right now and take the damn dog with you. And close your windows." And so, I told my son that it was okay, that everything was finally going to be okay and that he and Buddy just needed to wait upstairs and I would be home soon. And I just needed him to have everything ready. And he said, "I love you, Mom. I will." And then, you see, there was a line at the place and then, my credit card wouldn't work and it took longer than it should have, much longer. And by time I got back and I turned up our street, you see, I couldn't even get close to our house, there were so many cars and...

I parked, and I ran, and I could see. I wanted to close my eyes and just pretend it away. But I could see. Just as I see it now. Fire is everywhere now. Great tongues of red and awful orange fingers. Like the fire was hungry, consuming our little blue and white house, turning it black, eating it. This was our summer. And I tried. I tried to walk in, because if I couldn't just get in there, be there with him, hold him. I fought them so hard. But they wouldn't let me in. And so I screamed my son's name until all I could hear was the roaring.

Do you understand now? It needs red and orange to be finished. I can't finish it that way. They found my son upstairs, in the corner of his bedrooms. He was holding Buddy.

The windows in his room were already too hot to touch. But Buddy was there, with my boy. Buddy stayed with him, with my little boy. After John sent them upstairs he, um, he lit a cigarette and then, he, he just fell asleep. And John, he walked out the front door and he took that cold winter with him. While my boy was upstairs... So I paint him and I keep him with me that way. All that we had and all that we'll never have. If I paint his high school graduation, then there he is, cap and gown, and I'm in the bleachers, cheering. I paint him on his wedding day. He looks so handsome. I..I just needed another thirty minutes and then we were going to go away. Sometimes I wonder if we did and this is just another place that I don't really understand. An in-between place.

I, I don't even know what I'm saying anymore. I'm sorry that painting isn't for sale, but thank you for all your kind words. Maybe my son will stop by later. Maybe he'll bring Buddy. I wait, you see. I wait, and I wait and I wait. I'll wait forever until I get to see him again. But, for now, I keep a little piece of him with me until I get to see him again, you know? Until he shows up... After it happened, that thing I was talking about, I got to go and pick a few things up. Just a few. And, um, there was that tape recorder. The one I gave him for Christmas. And um, he'd recorded himself, and I listen to it now, anytime we're apart for a little while. I listen to it all the time, actually.

Hi Mom, it's me, your little monster. I thought it would be kind of cool to keep a record of stuff on here and maybe give it to you when I go away to college or something. So, today I wanted to say thank you for letting me keep Buddy. He says thanks for his neat blue collar. I know John hates him, but he's good to have around. John was better today, I know you feel bad, Mom, but it's not that bad. But if we ever do want to go away and planning out places we could go with the maps. You're better than a Mom and a Dad put together. Seriously. We'd be fine, I'd protect you. And that word I missed - it's palliate- it means, "to make a mistake better." I can spell it now. And I know you said you wouldn't be able to sing to me anymore when I leave him, but that's not true. I'll call you and you can, you can sing, "If you go out in the woods today, you're sure of a big surprise. For every bear that ever there was will gather there for certain, because today's the day the teddy bears have their picnic." Anyway, I love you, Mom. Don't worry so much about me.

THE INFLATABLE SHIP

A Poem
By Carl Sasoon

It was a lullaby she thought she'd
long forgotten, and she hummed so
quietly that she could only hear it in her head.
but there aren't any mockingbirds here for miles
and her shoes are all wrong and if a song could
save them, then she wouldn't be pacing around
sand dunes likes this, and if it's nine o'clock at
night, then the God-awful sun shouldn't be shining
this perilously bright, but no matter how daunting the
challenge, a watchful mother must always make it right.
what a time to get emotional or remember that you
forgot to turn off the oven or wish that he'd open his
mouth wider in order for you to step inside and find safety.
her lost daughter lies beyond the next dune.
how old was she when she lost her first tooth?
her little grown-up girl wallows in sand,
she sympathizes with snow, she knows.
she hasn't seen the ocean for months.

But i hate the ugly confines
of my watchtower, nothing more
than a horrible metaphor for the fact
that i'm scared of falling that many miles
into the wild abyss of bristling sand.
i hardly ever can comfort the way that i plan.
she uses brushes and i'm busy with keys,
i promise, i'm writing as fast as i can.
it is just not quickly enough and so i scream
through the lace of my hands.
i tell her it's coming, it's approaching,
a dark mass, a bad thing, sailing over
the expanse of the sand, a vessel, a
barge, something so large that i do not
know how many terrible things it carries inside.
i do not understand it, this awful maneuver, but i
know the inflatable ship is approaching,

and as certain as clockwork, i know they will harm.
from miles across the desert, she and i, we lock eyes,
if for only a moment, and in that quickfire instant
i realize that she knows it too.

This woman lies silent with beauty.
a patron of pocket-watches, she mixes
up colors, coaxing them gently onto bright
easels, squeezing out life that the others have missed.
the brushes she should have brought,
a portrait landscape she could have thought up
a million times into infinity and simply painted over
these silly square miles of sand. heavy sand.
hot sand. sand that demands that she just keep
on walking into the sun towards an unforgotten
daughter and she doesn't know which direction
the ocean claims to be going.

But i saw her last, back before this terrible blast.
we were at one of those things in Manhattan,
with everyone gathered to watch her big canvasses,
pictures in motion, moments not betrothed with
the hits and misses that others have had.
she introduced me, her beautiful blue man,
brought forth out of structure, out of spirit,
birthing a son that she had not had, but he
stepped out of the canvass and in to my hands.
He and I drank three bottles of Syrah that night,
a good one, from Sonoma, I think, and he tinkered
a little with my force-field I wanted, so badly, to yield
but it's never quite right to get involved with an
ultramarine man. she saw me the following morning,
shaking her head softly and laughing, knowing
that he'd already shrunk into a single dimension.
What a strange pick for a single night stand.

But too many new year's have passed since
that beautiful night and she's right, the brushes

just get lost under the dunes and her fingers are
too small to realign reality but her love is too tall
to fall back onto uncertainty or second guessing
or how the west wasn't really all that wild,
and I see from my difficult watchtower,
she's been working, her hands covered in paint
recounting in color every step taken by her
blindfolded daughter and hadn't she ought to
be able to paint every moment, every line,
every note, a psychic remote control sending
the same blaming message over and over:
this is what family does for each other-
and this was my daughter's first dawn,
initial steps, hold her close, let her go,
boys, but she's quiet, maybe too shy,
beautiful, talent unspoken, but we have
to protect her, it's raining too hard, she's
getting bigger, a sister, loyal, loves her father,
brave and afraid, came close to becoming a mother,
as close as touching the tip of a hurricane.
the undisputed thing about unconditional love
is that we own it and i know for certain that
this woman will find her daughter.

She will paint far into the darkness and i'm
typing as swiftly as possible, but fingers fallen
asleep from the weight of this task.
that dreadful thing is docked somewhere at
the edge of the hard horizon, waiting, just waiting
to sail through sand the moment we stop the creating.
paint, keep painting. my fingers exhausted from tapping.
only this birthing can keep the awful ship at bay,
holding an open space, an earmarked page,
to keep a small place for us because the desert
is just the same as this thing we call the world
and after this ship passes, there will be others,
but for certain we'll see them, standing like sentinels,
criticizing like simpletons, waiting patiently for the

daughter to return unharmed, whole, perfect only
because all of our flaws are so many,
and it is truly the inspiration, the art, the love,
that's able to keep the ship, the beast,
the evil at bay.

ABOUT THE AUTHOR

Angeline Brom graduates from Mills College in Oakland, California in May 2012. She is also the Creative Director for picketfenceforensics, a company dedicated to promoting excellence in high school forensics. Angeline spearheaded the development of Fast Horse Drama to promote expanded access to quality literature appropriate for short drama productions and competitive speaking. Angeline has performed numerous dramatic pieces in addition to coaching (and competing) at a national level in high school forensics. She lives, writes and works in Oakland, California.

12584496R00042

Made in the USA
Charleston, SC
14 May 2012